TAKE YOUR LIFE BACK FROM

FAMILIAR SPIRITS

ZION WILLINGHAM

ZION WILLINGHAM

Take Your Life Back From Familiar Spirits

This book is dedicated to my Lord and Savior Jesus Christ. I would also like to dedicate it to my son Judah. Finally, I would like to dedicate this book to everyone who has been affected by the evils of familiar spirits.

Contents

I

Isaiah 49:24-26

24 *Shall the prey be taken from the mighty, or the lawful captives delivered?*

25 *But thus saith the Lord, Even the captives of the mighty shall be taken away, and the prey of the terrible shall be delivered: for I will contend with him that contendeth with thee, and I will save thy children.*

26 *And I will feed them that oppress thee with their own flesh; and they shall be drunken with their own blood, as with sweet wine: and all flesh shall know that I the*

1

First Things First

If you have not given your life to Jesus Christ, familiar spirits have a covenant right to your life. Salvation renders that old covenant obsolete and grants you all of the rights to freedom that Jesus died for you to have. (Hebrews 8:13)

Repeat these prayers with me to start your journey to deliverance from familiar spirits.

Father, I cannot save myself. I know that without you I can never be who you ordained me to be. I need you. I confess that I am a sinner and I want to turn away from my sins Please help me to change the way I think and act. I receive you as my Lord and Savior. I thank you for the gift of salvation. Now I pray that you will fill me with the Holy Ghost so that I will receive the power to fight and overcome every familiar spirit that is laying claim to my life. I confess that I am free and righteous through your blood. In Jesus' name, I pray. Amen.

2

Introduction

What if what we've been taught about familiar spirits is incomplete or even completely incorrect. What if the work of these evil spirits is far more advanced than we ever imagined. Could the work of familiar spirits be the reason for the turmoil in your home, office, or church?

"Wisdom is the principal thing; therefore, get wisdom and in all thy getting, get understanding." (Proverbs 4:7) I've come to realize over the years that the most important movement in a Christian walk is a godly move towards knowledge. When we seek to get an understanding, we serve the God who promises to "give liberally and upbraid not." (James 1: 5-6) In simpler terms, he will give you as much understanding as you need, and not remove it from you or snatch it back. On the other hand, it's the job of familiar spirits to snatch the word from you and give you knowledge that binds you and steals your authority.

I suggest you read this book with a bible in your hand. Test every scriptural reference and word. The Bereans were applauded by Paul for being industrious in their careful study of the word.

Acts 17 "These were more noble than those in Thessalonica, in that they received the word with all readiness of mind, and searched the scriptures daily, whether those things were so. (12) Therefore many of them believed; also of honourable women which were Greeks, and of men, not a few." The word noble means "having or showing qualities of high moral principles or deeds. Simply put, Paul regarded the quality of the mindset of these men and women as higher than Thessalonica, by their willingness to hear the word and compare it with the scriptures. I have yet to find one situation that the Bible does not address with careful study. Mind you, some things are more directly covered than others, but ultimately the Bible is a living book designed to show us the way to salvation.

I would also suggest taking notes for further study. The bible states that in the multitude of counsel there is safety(Proverbs 15:22). The first counsel must always be the Word of God. The Bible says that three witnesses will establish a matter on earth. It is the water, the blood, and the Spirit.

Furthermore, three will testify and that is the spirit, water, and The blood. (1 John 5:8) Therefore, when there is a question we can trust the spirit, water, and the blood to testify to the truth of any matter.

I hope that you complete this book with a strong sense of understanding about the nature and danger of familiar spirits.

This book is not intended to ignite fear in your heart regarding familiar spirits. Quite the contrary. Fear will not accomplish anything in removing the harm these spirits have caused to your life. Instead, I hope to embolden you with scriptures to fight the good fight of faith.

The Bible is your Sword of the Spirit. It is only through the Word, the blood, and the Spirit that we can expect to contend with Familiar Spirits.

It is an aspect of our humanity that wisdom is often obtained by experience. Wisdom without an experience can result in favor without an explanation to maintain it. This explains why the fervent life and prayer characteristics of a person can bring naturally occurring blessings to later generations. These generations would enjoy the favor of generational blessings from their ancestors and assume it is simply good luck, when in all actuality they are enjoying the blessings that their ancestors worked to obtain.

Wisdom, conviction, and zeal are often built on an altar covered in the blood of a battle won. Solomon can attest to this. He was arguably the wisest man in the entire world, yet without the battle, scars to underwrite his character. Ultimately, with the help of thousands of wives and concubines, he had to learn in the classroom of battle the vanity of too many ill-advised marriages, extra-marital relationships, and the worst offense of idolatry and bloody witchcraft.

Familiar Spirits completed their operation of infiltrating the generational blessing handed down from David, and turning it into shame. (Psalm 4:2)

What does Solomon's abundance of wisdom and lack of understanding have to do with familiar spirits? Well, ultimately Solomon came to an understanding. He came into agreement with YAHWEH and put away idolatry. Likewise, you can do the same. Understand that these spirits may be guilty of so very many things, but ignorance is not one of those things. They are likely smarter, stronger, better equipped than you are for the battle. Their main advantage is that they often know you better than you know yourself, and they feel that they will be a better version of you than you can ever be. It is their main goal to occupy your territory and kill, steal, and destroy. These spirits are worse than other spirits because it is often difficult to separate their voice from your own. This means that these spirits have learned to talk like you, and reason to you so that you will be deceived to think that they are you. They are only interested in knowing how you think, to pervert your thinking with their suggestions. They are expert lawyers and fully know the extent of their legal rights, based upon your actions. They devote their time to gaining as many legal rights as possible. Fortunately for them and unfortunately for us, they often get the legal right they covet. They use this right to commit all sorts of actions on the unsuspecting man.

The biggest tragedy is that it is common to blame "God's will" for the activities of familiar Spirits and other spirits, while self-righteously presenting these accusations as faith. What an insult! For example, it's written," I would that thou would be in good health and prosper, even as your soul prospers"(3 John 1:2) and then something is happening that is seemingly contrary to is scripture. The person who was the recipient of the familiar spirit attack piously claims, "God knows all things." We just have to trust he knows what is best for us. Or the evil cousin of that cliché', "God works in mysterious ways, if Satan did it then God allowed it to happen". What utter rubbish! This is a misuse of the scripture "as far as the heavens are above the earth, is how far God's ways are above our ways" (Isaiah 55:9). Remember that the veil has been torn! Jesus wants us to take his yoke upon us and learn of him. If you learn someone then you know them. If you know him then you know and what he is not. When situations present themselves that do not have his fingerprint then we know it is from the enemy. We must arise and resist Satan and all of his devils at all times.

Satan is your enemy. You must become angry with Satan, get annoyed at his works, get biblical education and wisdom about his ways, and the operation of his kingdom. You have far superior weapons through the Holy Spirit, the blood of Jesus, and the Word of God.

Don't misunderstand me. Familiar spirits are very skilled foes. They know you. They want to be you and then destroy you. They have no problem using your weaknesses against you. If you tend to eat away your troubles, they will make sure the Krispy Kreme light is always on as you are driving home from a stressful day at work. Why? They do this because they know that when you overeat and commit the sin of gluttony, they have a legal right to attack you in other areas, and release demons who will continue to seek to open up as many legal access points as possible. So they hope you don't stop at one doughnut, but eat a full dozen doughnuts, and then go to bed so they can become a spirit husband and attack you in your dream. Cold right? This is the nature of your frienemy, familiar Spirits. The worst part of this scenario is that you may be completely oblivious to this chain of events. Does that mean that they are impossible to fight against? No. We serve a mighty God who is fully able to fight those things which occupy us and bring them under subjection to the true and living God.

Godly victories, as mentioned earlier, are often obtained only through a bloody battle. You must be ready to fight. If these spirits have taken up residence in your life, you must be determined that they cannot remain. These spirits have deceived even the elect, so you must be willing to constantly pray against deception. Everything that psychology has told you was a part of your "psyche" and just your "personality" must be discarded in favor of a renewed mind in Jesus Christ. You must be ready to put on the whole armor of God and determine that this day to recover yourself one step at a time.

Will it be easy? Probably not. Keep in mind that the most devious of human frienemies leave your presence at some time. They should sleep at some point. In contrast, these spirits never sleep. Worse, they consider you their house. They want to take over every aspect of your life and destroy it. They want to ensure that everything concerning your family is destroyed. They will, in some cases, pretend to be you, by speaking to your mind in the first person, and at the same time destroy everything that you were created to be. These spirits are so diabolical that they learn to mimic people and then return as the ghost of that person to enslave their children and continue the maniacal cycle. This cycle is often referred to as a generational curse. Who is the carrier of the curse? The familiar spirit. I liken familiar spirits to the family doctor who refers you to specialists to further their aim. For example, the familiar spirit monitoring you may open you up to anger and travel through your family line for an unlimited number of generations undiscovered. In this case, you will have generations of people who say things like, "our family is just like that." Other people may say things like, "you know that the Jones family is full of hotheads." The hothead is the familiar spirit who opened the door to anger many generations ago in Grandma and Grandpa Jones and then proceeded to stalk and deposit these spirits in the children. No one told the Jones children and descendants that this was not really who they were. There was no one to pull the cover off the real charlatan. So he continued his heinous assignment, undiscovered.

May this not be your situation today in the name of Jesus. Now that I have introduced you to who may arguably be your worst enemy, let's take a page from their playbook and do some intel on the activities of familiar spirits. The Holy Ghost will teach you many things about the work of these spirits in your life, your family, your church, your neighborhood, and even your country. The Bible exhorts us to be wise as a serpent (familiar spirit) and harmless as a dove (holy ghost). The Holy Ghost has the power and authority to destroy anything contrary but he operates with quiet wisdom as a gentleman.

Jesus said, I came to set a fire, but what will I if it is already kindled. (Luke 12:49) Who is the "I" in this sentence? It is the Holy Ghost fire. God knows when to slow burn and when to set an explosion. Wisdom and understanding will give you this same knowledge. If you are a child of the God of Elijah, the God of Abraham, Isaac, and Jacob. If you believe that Jesus is the son of God who is raised from the dead and that the Holy Ghost was poured out onto all flesh, congratulations, you are called. Answer the call of the end-times and enter into war against your worst enemy, the enemy who looks just like you

II

Ephesians 6:12

– For we wrestle not against flesh and blood, but against principalities, against powers, against the rulers of the darkness of this world, against spiritual wickedness in high [places].

3

The Work of Familiar Spirits

It is not unusual to discover the presence of familiar spirits after they have blocked, hindered, or sabotaged a life. In this case, it's more of a desperate attempt to figure out exactly what happened, than a simple desire for knowledge. This is indicative of the wicked nature of familiar spirits. They create so much havoc, yet they are extremely skilled at concealing their activities for many years. They may hide behind the sudden confusion in a home, infidelity, arguments, and even lack of marriage. These things are just life, right? Wrong! We are living in a generation where it is more common to use terms such as "let's not over-spiritualize things" than it is to seek out the whole of the matter. The truth is that the matter may be more spiritual than physical. How do we explain a man who has a beautiful wife at home, and suddenly "falls in love" with someone who cannot even hold a candle to his wife, and deserts his family? Only to attempt to return years later seemingly clueless about what made him make such an unwise decision. In later chapters, we will discuss the domino effect and how familiar spirits skillfully employ its use to cause mayhem. Likewise, we can use the same effect to advance the kingdom of God.

How They Hide

One of the most common ways that familiar spirits hide their peeping and

13

muttering is to embed their communications and evil transmissions in the thought patterns of their victims. In this, they can convince the victim that the thoughts are their thoughts. Often a person will become confused and even troubled or distressed by the thoughts that pass through their mind. The most vile act of these evil mental intruders is that they will then turn about and begin to accuse and blame the victim for a thought that they implanted. If the victim does not understand familiar spirits they will think that these thoughts are their own and become an open receiver of spirits of guilt and condemnation for a thought that never even originated with them in the first place. This is just the beginning of the mind games that these people play on unwitting victims, yet it is one of the most important because most attacks begin in the mind. 1 Romans 12:2 states "And be not conformed to this world: but be ye transformed by the **renewing of your mind**, that ye may prove what is that good, and acceptable, and perfect, will of God.

Logically it is easier to control anything when it is contained than when it is spread. Likewise, it is easier to form, execute, and monitor the effects of an attack on a victim from the inside out. These spirits will always attack your mind first because it just makes more sense to do so. The act of implanting thoughts and influencing the thoughts and actions of their victim is only one of their dirty mind tricks.

They will also implant images, ideas and even affect physical senses. Have you ever just had a bad mood. There is no explanation for the mood, everything just kind of sets you off. You don't realize that you've adapted your mind to integrating the internal speech into your thought pattern. In other words, it's not you. You are not having a bad mood. A very cunning person, in the form of a spirit, is manipulating your day to annoy you. This person has an agenda and it is best to figure this out quickly before they carry it out. This is where the scripture comes in. " Wherefore gird up the loins of your mind, be sober" (1 Peter 1:13). This scripture is written as a command which means that Jesus not only expects you to do it but you and only you, were given the legal authority to do it. He didn't say gird up the loins of your mind and that of your neighbor, kids, family, or even the family pet. He meant gird up your mind and be sober. So let us break this down a little further. Our friends at the Oxford dictionary define the term gird as (a person or part of the body) with a belt or band. A young man was to be girded with the belt of knighthood "secure (a garment or sword) on the body with a belt or band.

So we are to encircle with a belt or band the loins of our mind and be sober. Loins are "the seat of strength" for the believer. Therefore, we are to encircle the seat of the strength of our minds and be sober. Have you ever seen a drunk person try to reason or explain something? They might slur their words or lose focus. Likewise, we are to have a mind that is not drunk. It is quite clear that a drunk person is squarely under the control of a demonic spirit that induces drunkenness. Likewise, a person who is drunk from the "cares of this life" is often under the control of an evil spirit with an agenda. This agenda is simple, it is to kill, steal, and destroy. Therefore, Jesus exhorts us to encircle our minds and be sober and watch unto prayer.

Now we return to our example, you have a bad mood. Understand that there is a very cunning and deceptive person who is at the very least influencing the mood that you are currently experiencing. That means that whenever your coworker's loud laughter becomes dangerously annoying, the annoyance is a result of this spirit. High-pitched laughter aside, there is usually some bigger agenda connected to your bad mood.

I understand this may seem silly. I simply suggest you put life into perspective. Life is a series of individual days that can never be redone. There are no repeats. You may do the same thing for two days, but no two days are the same. This makes each day precious. Therefore an entire day in a bad mood is a major opportunity to spoil something precious while setting the groundwork to kill, steal, and destroy as much as possible from the victim's future. Satan and his kingdom know that Jesus' return is imminent, therefore they are keenly aware of the importance of each day.

We are to never simply accept a thought as "just how I think." If you are uncomfortable with the thought then you are not likely the source of such a thought. Is all of this confusing? Don't worry! The Bible did all of the legwork for us when it gave us an outline of the things we need to think about. Philippians 4:7 states "Finally, brethren, whatsoever things are true, whatsoever things are honest, whatsoever things are just, whatsoever things are pure, whatsoever things are lovely, whatsoever things are of good report; if there be any virtue, and if there be any praise, think on these things."

I heard a very famous deliverance minister say that if the thought is not one of these things then it is a sign of the presence of a demon. Likewise, if you are unable to redirect the thought to those things, or negative things continue to interrupt those things, deliverance is necessary. Remember we are to gird the loins of our mind. What do we gird, or encircle, it with? Philippians 4:6-9 gives great girding material.

Philippians 4:6 "Be careful for nothing, but in everything by prayer and supplication with thanksgiving let your requests be made known unto God"

If you are busy praying and making your prayer and supplication known unto God, it is difficult for a familiar spirit to manipulate your thoughts. At the very least, the wrong thoughts will stick out like a sore thumb, when measured against prayer and thanksgiving.

When you gird your mind with Philippians 4:6 then you should receive Philippians 4:7 "And the peace of God, which passeth all understanding, shall keep your hearts and minds through Christ Jesus." Why? Well anyone that has had a house full of noisy children can tell you that quietness after a busy and loud day can bring much relief to your ears. The effect is multiplied when you consider, the silencing of a stubborn demonic personality who loves to feed you negative information. Yet, Paul was not done in this prophetic revelation. The next scripture essentially states that if you do this, he will keep your heart and your mind sane, and ultimately give you peace and victory. "Those things, which ye have both learned, and received, and heard, and seen in me, do: and the God of peace shall be with you." Peace is a spirit. Angels are spirits. The Holy Spirit is a Spirit. The debate of whether or not demons are fallen angels is a dispute best saved for a future chapter. Here we are told that if we gird up the loins of our mind, that a spirit called the God of Peace, who is the Holy Ghost will be with you. Now let me draw a connection for you, the Bible states that "Now the Lord is that Spirit: and where the Spirit of the Lord is, there is liberty." What are you being liberated from? The person who captured your attention and who seeks to capture your mind through evil conversation. Therefore, a basic formula is (Philippians 4:6-7 + You = liberty from familiar spirits)

I mentioned earlier that this spirit has an agenda. This agenda is always to steal from you, kill you, and destroy you and everything connected to you. Today they want to just kill your mood or your blessings. This spirit may want you to negatively confess something about your day which stops a big blessing that was on the way or to give up on holiness and return to worldly ways. They may even want to shift your focus from God to some other method or make an ill-advised move. Whatever their aim, their motives are clear. I am convinced that every family has at least one familiar spirit. They move through the family line controlling and manipulating the health, wealth, and temperament of the members of the family. They may operate under such terms as genetic predisposition or even generational curses. These terms are both valid, the problem is that a familiar spirit is a person. This means that you don't just have a "curse" that invokes images of some sort of gray cloud with mysterious floating black material hanging over the head of individuals and creating all sorts of physical, mental, social, or emotional frustrations. Likewise, this situation is much greater than the positioning of chromosomes and DNA. If this were not true, how do we explain poverty that seems to travel from generation to generation? A person can blame a lack of responsibility with money on genetics, but how do you explain stubborn poverty and situations that arise in the lives of fiscally responsible individuals with no logical explanation. Family members who have never met each other, yet suffer the same malady.

A familiar spirit may place a curse or create havoc as a result of legal rights you or your ancestors have given, but make no mistake the aggressor in the situation is always the familiar spirit. These spirits follow the parents then monitor and groom the kids. They interfere and even assign other spirits to interfere with the children. They then monitor the grandchildren. Wash, rinse, and repeat. Can you imagine telling a brand new mother who is busy monitoring every drop of dirt that enters the room that her precious baby is being monitored by an evil spirit? The conversation may go something like, "sorry, your baby may be clean, but a fallen angel is monitoring your child to make sure your baby never becomes a doctor." Make it worse and console her by saying, "Don't worry, you will have another child and this spirit will monitor and ensure that your second child will never be an accountant." This is a somewhat exaggerated example, but in the spiritual realm, this is what happens when many babies are born. A new mother can never imagine that she would have an invisible person monitoring her that will physically or spiritually attack her children when they make movements towards the career field that God intended for their life. By now you may be saying "don't you think this is a bit extreme?" My answer is simple, visit a deliverance minister and ask them to share some stories. Countless stories of stolen and exchanged glory, sabotage, and harassment from the kingdom of darkness.

I would even go so far as to argue that the work of familiar spirits makes up at least 50% of deliverance cases. Why? The reason is simple, they know you best.

4

Who Are Familiar Spirits

It is commonly believed that familiar spirits are the lower-level demons involved in the harassment of a person. It is largely because they often possess animals, that they have been mistakenly characterized as pets. They are also referred to as slave spirits. This is deception. People who give themselves over to be possessed by demons quickly discover that possession means to own. These spirits have no intention of being a slave to any human.

Familiar Spirits are fallen angels. They are the direct opposites of your guardian angel and will contend with angels on issues of legal rights. These spirits are the organizer of most, if not all, evil attacks. They are usually marine spirits and often work in conjunction with other marine spirits. This should come as no surprise. Our bodies consist of 80 percent water.

The United States Geological Survey reports that "About 71 percent of the Earth's surface is water-covered, and the oceans hold about 96.5 percent of all Earth's water. Water also exists in the air as water vapor, in rivers and lakes, in icecaps and glaciers, in the ground as soil moisture and in aquifers" (usgs.com, 2020) The Bible mentions marine spirits such as Leviathan, Dagon, Rahab, and of course Python throughout the old and new testament. The marine kingdom requires in-depth coverage, beyond what I will give in this book. Suffice to know that monitoring is a huge component of their duties.

Who was the first Familiar Spirit named in the Bible? None other than Satan himself. Satan monitored Adam and Eve. He knew full well what would happen when Adam and Eve ate the fruit. Satan also knew that for Adam and Eve to "be as gods and know the difference between good and evil" would be a demotion as man had, and now has through Jesus, authority in the earth that superseded that of angels.

Scriptural References
    Genesis 2:7
    Genesis 3:4
    Psalm 8:4-8
    Isaiah 14:12-16

Who They Are Not

Familiar spirits are not, or at least should not be your husband, best friend, boyfriend, confidant, protectors, guardian, or guide. Do some of these terms sound familiar? Familiar spirits have managed to be classified under many terms. These terms are more of a term for the role that the familiar spirit plays than an actual definition of the demon.

Spirit Husbands- There are scores of books, articles, and sermons written about spirit husbands. New revelations about the work of spirit husbands are being released regularly. A familiar spirit attaches itself sexually to its "host" and engages in a spirit marriage. The result is usually spirit children and increased bondage in the spirit realm. The natural results are sudden and inexplicable poverty, no marriage or terrible trouble in the marriage, natural children being pursued and repeatedly attacked spiritually and even physically, physical health ailments including fibroids and excessive bleeding. They have been known to torment, torture, or even kill a partner or potential partner. Note that it has been revealed recently that spirit husbands can also be human beings operating through black magic who, for whatever reason, want to ensure their target remains alone. They may have some sort of attraction to the individual or some other reason to commit these abominable acts. Either way, their black magic is facilitated by demons therefore if a human being is committing evil activities such as projecting into dreams and astral attacks, they are likely operating on some level through the work of familiar spirits.

I have never seen Twilight and I have no intention of seeing it. This being said, I have seen the frenzy that it has sparked. Certainly, some people were happy to see on the big screen, what they had been participating in for generations. Familiar spirits are not your friends. If you are a human being then Satan has one and only one goal towards you and your destiny, it is to kill, steal, and destroy. He is not your friend. Demons are not your friends. They may feign concern for your wellbeing and pretend to want the best for you. This is deception. These spirits are simply illustrating the adage, "keep your friends close, your enemies closer." They are going to follow you whether you are hostile or hospitable towards them. They are there to do a job. Their job is to monitor, create legal rights, assist you into entering into harmful covenants, deceive you into making bad decisions, and bring all manner of torment in your life while creating open doors for any demons that will further their cause. These "friends" will also set in place the bondage for your children and future generations. Ultimately, they are on assignment to kill, steal and destroy. If you must make friends with someone who cannot be seen, improve your life and make sure it is the Holy Spirit.

Spiritual boyfriends/girlfriends act very similar to spirit husbands, wives. They may marry you or they may just enter and attack you sexually. They may not interfere with your marriage, but they will cause all sorts of trouble with fidelity and sexual interest. Why? Well, it could be that they want to encourage negative sexual behavior or they may seek to eventually cause a divorce. They may also try to separate a family to expose the children.

The work of confidant, guardian, protector and guide belongs to the Holy Ghost. Familiar spirits seek to fill the void. They will validate you and excuse behavior that the Holy Ghost condemns, and once you have committed the act, turnaround and condemn you for the same behavior. They hope to make you grieve the Holy Ghost so that he does not have direct control over your actions, and to pull you deeper into bondage. They are happy to attack your enemies when it suits them in exchange for your allegiance to their witchcraft. They will also separate you from family and friends to gain control over you. I believe that when someone plans to attack a person with witchcraft they first locate the family witch who in turn consults the familiar spirit assigned to that person to organize and receive authorization for the attack. Then this" friend," the familiar spirit, oversees the execution of the attack. This is happening all while this person may feel that this spirit is a friend.

While this has not been verified, it has even been reported by pastors that astral projection is simply the implantation of images by demons. This means that a person never really travels, the demon travels and implants the pictures. Whether this is true or not remains to be seen, but it does illustrate the manipulation and abilities of these cunning individuals.

Ghosts- Familiar spirits are the perfect "ghosts". Who can imitate a person better than someone who is around a person night and day, monitoring their every move? They will often appear and torment the living family members with the image of the person. One deliverance minister reported questioning the "ghost" of a man's dead wife only to discover that this "ghost" did not know the answer to key questions that were being asked. This just goes to show that even the best imitation is still an imitation. No one, even wicked spirits, can know everything about a person.

5

Anatomy of an Abuser

What makes a man pursue a woman relentlessly with an abusive intent in mind. This man, once he has married, or conquered, this woman will begin to beat and go on a one-man wrecking campaign to destroy her self-esteem. He is slow and methodical about his abuse. Slowly introducing her to the cycle of abuse. One abuse at a time, he begins to condition her to be abused. It may begin as mental abuse, sly comments, or cutting words. It slowly escalates to physical abuse. They then enter into the cycle of building up, violent outbursts, remorse, and then building again.

What happened? A practical person would ask," if you wanted a punching bag, why search for a woman? Could you not join the gym? The question is, what is the payoff? It may seem crass but it bears asking. For his part, he may not understand the strong witchcraft and deception spirits involved in physical and mental abuse to this level. Further, he may have seen these things growing up and not understood that a generational curse is a spirit that travels from generation to generation. He cannot put into words the fact that he knew on the first date that he planned to beat this woman and eventually conquer her. He won't have the words to explain why beating her until she is deformed makes him feel better. The reason is simple, there is a very evil spirit who is on an assignment to destroy both his life and the life of his wife. Abusive spouses generally die before their spouses, which means this spirit accomplished its mission.

This is made worse if the wife also has a spirit husband. That means that both the husband and the wife have familiar spirits claiming both the husband and the wife as a spouse. They will often view the husband and wife as a rival and therefore seek to destroy them. This spirit will work through witchcraft and cause a man to physically abuse his wife and children. Likewise, a spirit husband will sabotage the human husband and seek to destroy the marriage.

Fear is a major driving force in all abusive relationships. Fear from the abuser and fear from the abused. Fear is a major principality that oversees many facets of the satanic kingdom. In this case, fear needs to exist in the abuser to drive them to abuse. It also needs to exist in the abused to freeze them in place to experience the abuse. If either end fails to operate according to fear the situation changes and becomes less habitable for fear. An abuser may physically deform their partner because they are afraid of losing them. They may also secretly not feel that they measure up and therefore they want to even the playing field. It is not uncommon to find an abuser who behaves in this manner intending to maintain control over their victim. It is essentially an " I keep them below me so that I can control them." Abusers do not always beat, they have several methods for maintaining control of their victim. This is the spirit of Pharoah. The Spirits of deception about the intention of the Children of Israel, and witchcraft drove Pharoah to refuse to allow the Children of Israel to go and worship God. This same spirit drove Pharoah in pursuit as they escaped.

Take the woman who berates her husband because of his weight. She insists that he is a fat slob. In her opinion, he is slow and useless and could care less about his health. She parades around in her jogging suits and constantly compares him to other men. When he eats she feigns utter disgust. He eats too fast and entirely too much. How useless! He is thankful that his wife, "stands by him." After all, what would he do without her? One day, despite his wife's daily tirade, he decides he is done with his weight problem. He immediately informs his wife that he will not be eating with the rest of the family tonight, as he plans to change his eating habits.

His wife seems surprised. Yet he is somewhat taken aback at the annoyed expression on her face. That night she makes his favorite dinner, a huge steak with his best dessert, and hands him a plain lettuce salad. She proceeds to eat the steak slowly in his presence. Despite this, he manages to hold his willpower. Once again, he notices displeasure on her face. Days pass and this continues every night until he gives up his diet. Soon he is back in the same habit of bad eating and his wife is back in the same habit of mental and verbal abuse. What happened? The minute the husband removed the tool from the wife's hands, the conditions for fear were shifted.

In this case, whether intentional or unintentional, the wife is practicing witchcraft against her husband. If he continues in the same direction we can certainly expect the situation to escalate. A study of abusers is necessary to understand some of the methodology and driving forces behind demons, and in particular familiar spirits.

They are the textbook parasite. Everything they do is to gain entrance, impose their will, and then gain control. Once in control, they do everything to keep their control. Their ultimate goal is to kill, steal, and destroy. Their immediate goal is to gain control, institute fear, anger, and frustration.

The easiest way to explain the environment in which familiar spirits thrive would be a comparison with the ecosystem we enjoy. Fear would be the oxygen that familiar spirits need to live and maintain a habitation to thrive. Frustration would be the sunlight which provides many health benefits while making a way for the familiar spirits to exist in the best possible environment. Anger is the water that familiar spirits need to function. If you remove any of these factors and you become less hospitable to the familiar spirit.

What does this mean? It means that we can compare the work of familiar spirits in a person's life, to that of a human spaceship that lands on Jupiter. The environment of Jupiter is not naturally conducive for a human being to live, therefore they must manipulate the atmosphere, and install their external artificial mechanisms to survive.

Likewise, a familiar spirit needs fear, anger, and frustration to survive. They cannot and will not live in an environment that is stable, happy, healthy, and whole. These environments are not suitable for their survival, thus they work to change the atmosphere of a person's life and install their external survival mechanisms to survive.

For example, they enter into a happy marriage and begin to peep and mutter to one spouse that the other may be cheating.

If this spouse does not understand that this voice is demonic and they yield to it, then the spirit of suspicion has a legal entrance. Unfortunately, in the arena of marriage, suspicion operates on the "where there is smoke there is fire" principle and may bring a real spirit of infidelity into the marriage causing one or both partners to cheat. This couple may be completely unaware of the demonic meetings and careful planning that was undertaken to create a suitable environment for demonic activity. These spirits are happy if the couple never discovers this fact because they will continue to introduce spirits into the lives of this couple and eventually try to kill, steal, and destroy the marriage. They will do this because the environment has been altered for their survival. On the other hand, if the person resists the devil and the devil flees she may be blissfully unaware of the pitfall created by the demons. For their part, the demons have been resisted and the environment is not suitable for their environment, so they will flee. Please note that this does not mean that the same demon will not come back over and over to try to regain entrance into the marriage and create a suitable environment for their survival.

Matrix

   A matrix is defined as "an environment or material in which something develops; a surrounding medium or structure."(Oxford 2019)' Put down your red and blue pill, they will not be needed for this truth. The God matrix is often referred to as the "invisible kingdom of God". In this kingdom exists the fruits of the spirit, godly love, and trust. The things that bring you closer to God are the things that exist in this matrix. Most have heard Christian brothers and sisters speaking of living in the "invisible kingdom of God, here on earth." This is what they mean. In the God matrix, the heavens are open and blessings come easily. Familiar spirits cannot survive in this kingdom. The light is too bright and they would be destroyed if they do not leave.

There is another matrix that I refer to as the FAF. The FAF matrix consists of fear, anger, and frustration. In this matrix, holy angels do not often operate because it has been optimized for demons and other wicked personalities. A person who lives in this matrix will often find the heavens closed and a strong "ministry" of familiar spirits. This is why we should never envy the workers of darkness. It was revealed to me that demons need the FAF matrix to survive. Therefore, those who intentionally invoke familiar spirits in themselves will also live constantly in a matrix of fear, anger, and frustration. This is not a personal thing. The demons will do anything to survive and a willing vessel to a demon will always get more than they asked for. This means that, even in their own lives, the familiar spirits will make sure that those who work iniquity are always at some level miserable.

This includes the rich. How can I be so sure? It's not because I am passing judgment. It's simply a matter of survival. The familiar spirits and other demons must have fear, anger, and frustration to survive. Therefore, they will manipulate the lives of their willing or unwilling hosts to ensure this environment is always met. Satan and his demons torment the people they occupy and especially those who intentionally align themselves with him. Thus proving the scripture, "the blessing of the Lord makes one rich and adds no sorrow"(Proverbs 10:22). Do not expect this to be a widely spread fact. It is quite the contrary. Everywhere we look, especially in the western world witchcraft and Satan are glorified. This is one of many deceptions. My brother and sisters run for your life. Escape the snares of the fear, anger, and frustration matrix. Everlasting life is worth everything.

So to continue with the Matrix theme, there will be no red or blue pill. Instead, praise God, there is the red blood of Jesus. There is also the fact that many are "asleep", to the truth of Jesus Christ. There is purposeful programming of unbelief in Jesus Christ that prevents many people from walking in the God matrix. Usually, it takes some sort of supernatural experience or real engagement against the kingdom of darkness to prompt a person to a real belief in Jesus Christ. In addition to the lack of belief in Jesus Christ, the average person also does not truly believe in Satan. I believe this was deliberate and has worked with unfailing results. The church uses terms like "that old devil", which makes him sound like a cartoon character. I am unhappy to report that Satan is a real person. He is not a red cartoon character with horns and a pitchfork. He is a real being who is evil and truly wants the worst for you. He has a real kingdom that is home to many of the rich and powerful people in this world. They will do what he says without question.

How they Enter

Familiar spirits enter much easier than most people can imagine. It can be as simple as watching a television program, reading a news article, or viewing social media. I run the risk of sounding like a fanatic and I do not care. The bible is clear "Regard not, those who have familiar spirits. Neither seek after wizards to be defiled by them: I am the Lord." (Leviticus 19:31). This includes television, radio, social media, websites, newspapers, and anywhere else where the "corrupt communication" of familiar spirits is found. (Ephesians 4:29–32) Serious Christians are beginning to discover that familiar spirits, water spirits, witchcraft spirits, and the power of the air hold an iron grip on popular culture. It may be easier to find a needle in a haystack than to find a movie that is not written by, dedicated to, and encoded with familiar spirits and other harmful demons. Children's movies and cartoons have not escaped the influence of these evil spirits, and are often programmed with harmful subliminal messages. We have to exercise caution with everything that we encounter. The key is to pray continually over all things we view. Try to avoid as much demonic influence in the things that we consume, and try to create an environment that is violently hostile to demonic entrance. This means that if they find their way in, they quickly discover that you are not a suitable environment to stay. Regular prayer will help to dislodge and cast out these spirits, or resist these spirits so that they will flee.

6

Witchcraft

Witchcraft and familiar spirits go together like peanut butter and jelly. One needs the other to operate. Rest assured you have a witch in your community, your neighborhood, family and you could have a witch or wizard in your church or even your home. Witchcraft is the end-time religion of the Antichrist and has quietly hijacked many churches. Current Christianity has created a comfortable environment for those involved in all forms of the occult and witchcraft to practice their craft while occupying key positions in the church. The result is a mix of idolatry which makes some churches very dangerous places for the spiritually wounded. We will discuss this later in the chapter.

What is witchcraft

Witchcraft at its core is a work of the flesh. The Bible says "Now the works of the flesh are manifest, which are these; Adultery, fornication, uncleanness, lasciviousness, Idolatry, witchcraft, hatred, variance, emulations, wrath, strife, seditions, heresies, envyings, murders, drunkenness, revellings, and such like: of the which I tell you before, as I have also told you in time past, that they which do such things shall not inherit the kingdom of God." (Galatians 5:19-21). This means that witchcraft is in the unregenerate personality of every human being.

The word witch derives from the word Wicca which means "to bend". A person does not necessarily need to issue an official curse or use some supernatural power to perform witchcraft. The best description of witchcraft is to manipulate someone else to do what you want to be done while making them believe that they want to do it. When we view it from this angle, we see how deeply rooted witchcraft is in our culture.

Example

A mother grabs the groceries out of the car and begins to carry them into the house with ease. She spots her 17-year-old son playing basketball and feels he should help carry in groceries. She adjusts her route to cross in front of his view and begins to limp. She limps more and more with each step. Her son spots mom limping with groceries and rushes over grabs the groceries from her hand and takes them into the house. The mother continues the pretense of limping and enters the house. When her son disappears back outside to continue his game, she straightens her steps and smiles that she "helped" her son understand that he should assist in bringing in groceries.

Let's say a deliverance minister informs the mother that she is indeed performing witchcraft against her son. She replies, "I have to, if I don't he sulks and complains every time I ask him to help me bring in the groceries." In this case, the deliverance minister would probably inform her that her son is also using witchcraft. He knows that if he behaves in a certain manner, it will dissuade his mother from requesting his assistance. He has learned the right words and mannerisms to influence his mother to behave in a certain manner while leaving her believing that it was her idea. No, he is not a wizard by spirit, but witchcraft is a work of the flesh.

It would certainly seem that a spirit of witchcraft has entered the home and has bound the members of the home. It would also seem that this spirit seeks to pollute the relationship between mother and son. It would be no surprise to find "innocent" movies about witches, television shows, books, or other items in the house. The family might also have candles and other items that witchcraft spirits love to inhabit in their home. Spiritual house cleansing can facilitate deliverance from familiar spirits. This may involve prayers and the removal of objects which may serve as open doors to evil spirits.

The fact that no spells or curses were issued does not change the spirit at work. This family would need deliverance from familiar spirits. Who whispered in the mother's ear, "limp and cross in his path"? Who whispered to the son, "huff and puff if she asks you to do anything, and she won't keep asking"? The answer is a familiar spirit. The same spirit that operates in someone who knowingly practices black magic, can also operate in the same manner in someone who practices unintentional or fleshly witchcraft.

Witchcraft is also a very in-depth subject that I will not cover extensively in this book. This topic tends to take over a book and we want to focus on familiar spirits. Suffice to know that witchcraft of all types will open your home to many problems. This is magnified when witchcraft is intentionally performed. The intentional practice of witchcraft has many negative consequences for future generations.

One such consequence is that it is also a surefire way to install ancestral spirits and generational curses in a family. These spirits may follow all of the family members for hundreds of years after the witch has died. In addition, these spirits may react violently to any member of the family who later decides to give their life to Jesus Christ. Imagine a practicing witch dies in 1971, yet in 2010 her great-great-granddaughter cannot keep a relationship and experiences disappointment and frustration in many areas in her life. She may also have strange health afflictions that seem resistant to all medication. This is due to the familiar spirit traveling through her family line. Yes, those familiar spirits which Hollywood has romanticized are evil demons that have an evil eye for your child. They will claim ownership over an entire family unless they are stopped. Unlike other spirits, familiar spirits will fight viciously to maintain their stronghold in a family.

Acts 16:16 presents a very detailed account of Apostle Paul's encounter with

Python.   There was a damsel possessed with the spirit of Python.   Her handlers followed her and monitored her closely. You must understand that they were not watching for her good, but their own financial benefit. They were communicating mind control commands to the Python spirit. Satan commissioned a complicated spy network of fallen angels, demons, and human agents. We know that he compensated the mind control handlers very well, by the fact that they were furious with Paul for setting free their income source.

The Python later took revenge

"And when her masters saw that the hope of their gain was gone, they caught Paul and Silas, and drew them into the marketplace unto the rulers, o the marketplace unto the rulers, And brought them to the magistrates, saying, These men, being Jews, do exceedingly trouble our city,

And teach customs, which are not lawful for us to receive, neither to observe, being Romans. And the multitude rose together against them: and the magistrates rent off their clothes, and commanded to beat them.

And when they had laid many stripes upon them, they cast them into prison, charging the jailor to keep them safely:"

34

A popular preacher noted that Paul was taken to the marketplace. Have you heard anything about greedy corporations manipulating the masses? There is nothing new under the sun.

They sent the girl to infiltrate and derail the church. Every week unrepentant servants of the kingdom of darkness enter churches with the same assignment. They use various nefarious methods to waylay the church and initiate Christians into witchcraft.

There are two takeaways and one bit of advice from this scripture.

1. The entire mind control handler scenario is not new. (There is more to say about this issue than can be covered in this book.)

2. Infiltration by the kingdom of darkness into the church is also an old concept. This explains some of the strange doctrines that have entered the church.

I advise anyone helping a person cast out a Python spirit to examine themselves and ensure there are no weak areas in their hedges. There have been several reports of Python spirits attacking deliverance workers who free their victims. Success boils down to knowledge. Weak serpent-handling usually occurs when there are weak spots in the believer's hedge of protection and a lack of knowledge.

Examples of weak serpent handling.
    Acts 16:16
    Genesis 3:1-6
    Job 3:1-26

Examples of strong serpent-handling
    Matthew 4
    Acts 28:1-5
    Revelation 11:4-6

In the case of the damsel in Acts 16:16 we see one of many attempts to waylay the church. When serpents operate in a ministry unhindered they will suffocate the anointing and create a cold environment in which they can survive. They do not enjoy operating alone, so their next order of operations is to fill the church with other agents until Satan's agenda for the ministry is fulfilled. This agenda does not end with the church. They seek out industries, governments, organizations, and groups. This explains why there is so much satanic symbolism in products. These agents are your bosses, neighbors, bankers, community leaders, or even the teachers in your child's school. Many children are initiated into witchcraft by this very method. They are the faithful, diligent, and hardworking church members who sit in the front pew each Sunday. They may be a mother or father of the church. Yet, they may be the person sidetracking the church, engineering divorce for the members, and attacking their finances.

Major decisions are made between the hours of 11 pm and 4 am. This means that many hours before a board meeting commences a group of fallen angels, demons, and evil people would have met to decide the outcome of the meeting during the hours of the night. You must meet with the Holy Spirit, his holy angels, and the Word of God to override evil decisions.

This is not a new phenomenon Micah 2:1 says "Woe to them that devise iniquity and work evil upon their beds! when the morning is light, they practice it, because it is in the power of their hand." The truth of the matter is that every person who intends to make their mark in life will need some sort of spiritual assistance. This intervention will either come from the kingdom of God or the kingdom of Satan. Therefore it stands to reason that if you are competing against a coworker for a promotion, and you spend three minutes praying before bed plus thirty seconds praying over food while your competitor spent a solid week sleeping in the graveyard, they may prevail. Familiar Spirits work best in cold environments. On the other hand, if this familiar spirit meets fire, you can prevail.

Witchcraft is a very in-depth topic that requires much greater study than I will cover here. Suffice to know three facts.

1. There are conscious and unconscious witches. Therefore never use the specific name of a suspected witch on your anti-witchcraft prayer.

2. Witchcraft will force you to take a strong look at your prayer life.

3. A witch or wizard who knowingly practices witchcraft may be completely consumed with the familiar spirit they invited into them. This spirit needs energy and will consume the person it inhabits. Christians receive our spiritual energy from the Holy Spirit, so always keep your eyes on him.

8. Unless God instructs you, never openly confront a witch. This is for two reasons.

The first is that they will rarely confess. They are sworn to carry this secret to their graves.

The second is that they won't stop attacking you. You can beg them with tears. You can even beg on your knees. It will not change their mind. Remember that familiar spirits take over the soul increasingly when witchcraft is intentionally practiced. Even family or friends who are witches and wizards will continue their activities. Pray for their salvation but remember that your number one requirement is to carry out your mandate in God. Contrary to what you may have been taught, Jesus takes no pleasure in the death of the wicked, but he takes less pleasure in the preponderance of evil over the lives of the righteous and those who seek the Lord. Please read Acts 13:10. I heard a preacher once note that this scripture was written by the same writer who wrote 1 Corinthians 13. Forgive those who practice witchcraft, love, and seek peace with all men but remember your first call as a Christian is to their victims. (Matthew 10)

Witchcraft has become an epidemic. The tentacles reach into every industry, family, and community. There are even reports of babies and small children holding roles in the coven. Powerful familiar spirits attach to these children and begin to fragment and consume such children early while using them to carry out heinous mandates.

Witchcraft runs deep in many homes, families, and communities. People involved in witchcraft make perfect church members. They are prompt, faithful, intelligent, and often the heads in their industry. They will usually take an interest in the prayer and fasting of the church to attempt to hinder or stop it altogether. They will also position themselves close to the Pastor in an attempt to attack or initiate the family. It is also very common for witches to attempt to gain access to children and initiate them or worse. This is why we must teach our children to pray over their food and open up about their experiences. Witchcraft pastors and church leaders will often overstep personal boundaries. They may demand information that you are not comfortable giving to them. They may use psychic witchcraft and call it prophecy. You must be watchful because many saints have been initiated in church. What a pity to discover that out of 100 church members you are the only one who is not a practicing witch or wizard.

Many books will give you knowledge and strategies when dealing with witchcraft. The key is to understand that no one has the right to use controlling tactics, even in the church.

A best practice is to always seek the face of God, who is the revealer of all things.

7

A Chain Effect

Nothing just happens. Everything that you have ever done, thought, or believed is a result of a carefully constructed chain. We choose the manufacturer of the chain. The manufacturers are Jesus or Satan. Each day we are adding, subtracting, and manipulating links to the chain that affects more than we could ever imagine. Familiar Spirits know that we don't take these things seriously. Let's look at one chain. Bob and Linda have a solid one-year-old marriage. The newlyweds have been anxiously awaiting a baby. Unbeknownst to them Bob's mother is not happy with her new Christian daughter-in-law and blames her for the loss of control of Bob and his finances. Bob was unaware that his dear mother is a witch. The scripture is clear that a man leaves his mother and cleaves to his wife. (Ephesians 5:31) Yet Bob's attachment to his mother causes disagreements which Linda seeks to avoid. In their church, they are taught that spiritual warfare is not biblical, and instead, they should pray blessings on their enemies. Linda has never heard a sermon about prayer. Instead, every sermon discusses forgiveness and prosperity. Linda has managed to avoid an overnight visit from Bob's mother, but finally, Bob allowed it without his wife's knowledge. Bob's mother did more than make Linda feel unwelcome in her own home, she also left powerful charms in the house for monitoring and manipulating the young couple.

The familiar spirit enters the home through the charms left by Bob's mother.

The couple begins to argue almost immediately after Bob's mother leaves. Things begin to disappear only to inexplicably reappear in different locations in the house. In addition, the couple both started to experience nightmares.

Suddenly Bob's eyes begin to wander as Linda experiences increased perverse dreams and physical maladies. It does not take long for the marriage to land on the rocks headed for divorce. How many marriages have ended through familiar spirit intervention?

It does not have to be a family member involved in witchcraft. It can be a cursed house, bad friends, coworkers, or just a cold environment. Remember the job of a familiar spirit is always to create a suitable environment.

To further explain the link, let's say Linda has a fire baptized, Holy Ghost-filled co-worker named Beth. They are not close friends, in fact, they rarely see each other. During her family's prayer time, the Holy Spirit ministers to Beth that Linda's home had suffered an arrow of darkness, and to see intercede for her. Beth obeys the Holy Ghost and fervently intercedes for Linda's family. This results in Linda feeling a strong desire to read her Bible. The terrible dreams begin to get better and she feels the urge to visit a local church that practices deliverance. Sensing her hold lifting, Bob's mother increases her efforts. The familiar spirit attacking the family increases its activity against Bob, as Linda has become a challenge. Bob becomes sullen and disinterested in his home and begins to date other women. It looks bad for the couple, but remember the prayers of Beth. Suddenly Bob finds a tract about hellfire on his desk at work and becomes pricked in his heart.

The scales seem to fall from his eyes as he joins his wife in a new Christian walk and becomes filled with the Holy Ghost. Fast forward five years and Bob and Linda now have three children and a happy home. The glory of God is upon their lives. Bob's mother confesses and receives deliverance and salvation. The salvation of an entire family was counted to Beth, who has no idea of the specifics of the problem or even the outcome. She is simply obedient to God.

The results are more than she could have ever imagined. Familiar Spirits know the power of prayers and the chain reaction created in the spirit. They seek to counter it with a negative and perverted chain that destroys lives.

The Chain Illustrated

The chain effect can occur on an intimate level, in which it seems to only affect you, my brother and my sister please believe that what you do always affects someone else. There is no such thing as a decision in a vacuum. For example, a woman who commits herself to God and waiting on the Lord may miss the man that familiar spirits have chosen to meet her in a nightclub, due to her walk with God. It seems that she only helped herself but, in all actuality, her children will be positively affected by her decision. People around her may also be positively affected by her decision. People whom she witnesses will also be positively affected by her position. Finally, someone watching her to see if "Christians are all hypocrites" will be positively affected

On the other hand, if she tires of waiting on the Lord, and listens to the familiar spirit who tells her that going to a nightclub is harmless, she will suffer. A person who planned to go to church could see her in the nightclub and decides Christians are all hypocrites. The man, sent from the devil, meets the woman in the nightclub and they become involved. He ultimately destroys the life of this woman with a sexually transmitted disease due to his promiscuous lifestyle. Her future plans of having children are dashed, as it is risky to have children. She may lose many years. Will God forgive her? Yes! Yet she will have missed out on many opportunities at the perfect will of God for her life. Maybe you have missed it. There is no time like the present to change the source of your chain. A pastor once said that prayer is one of the most powerful forces on the earth and prayers never die. You don't have to be an internationally renowned evangelist to change your life, and the lives of others through prayer. It does not matter how far down the wrong road you have gone. Your life will change today in the name of Jesus.

Repeat these prayers

Father in the name of Jesus, I ask that you will thwart the activities of familiar spirits in my life, the lives of my loved ones, and my community. You said in Leviticus 19:31 "Regard not them that have familiar spirits, neither seek after wizards, to be defiled by them: I am the LORD your God." I receive your word and pray that your Holy Spirit will reveal to me any area in which I am listening to the voice of familiar spirits.

Now, familiar spirit Matthew 16:19 says "I will give you the keys of the kingdom of heaven; whatever you bind on earth will be [a] bound in heaven, and whatever you loose on earth will be [b] loosed in heaven." I am a child of God. I take my key and I bind you and your activities in my life and the life of everyone connected to my chain. I release the anointing to break every yoke that your evil activities have integrated into my timeline and I decree a shift to the chain of events ordained by God for my life. In Jesus' name, I pray.

Believe this prayer with all of your heart. Your life will change. Your story has already changed. The mystery of faith is that faith is the substance of things hoped for. Therefore hoping in God yields faith. Remember faith without works is dead. What works? Prayer Works! This is another example of a godly chain. Holy hope leads to prayer and prayer leads to faith. Praise God that faith leads to an entirely different chain of events. Spend some time praising the Lord that you will fulfill the will of God for your life. We will discuss your future steps in the next chapter.

8

The Responsible Believer

So what to do? You realize that a familiar spirit has infiltrated your life and caused many problems. You may already be scrolling local deliverance ministries for a way out. Not so fast. I preface this statement with the understanding that it may be controversial and I respect anyone's right to disagree. If you are currently being attacked by familiar spirits and you are not in a church, unless you know the pastor or church leader or have a trusted person who can vouch for their stand in God, do not join a church just yet.

Countless people have entered churches broken searching for solutions only to be directed to the wrong church by familiar spirits and even attacked by witchcraft in the church. In my opinion, this does more harm than good. Likewise, if the familiar spirit attacking you is sent by witchcraft or evil family covenants, they will follow you to church and attempt to make you give up on God altogether. Familiar Spirits can possess anyone who yields themselves to be used, which means you must be a responsible believer.

What is a responsible believer? This is a believer who embodies Philippians 2:12 "***Wherefore, my beloved, as ye have always obeyed, not as in my presence only, but now much more in my absence, work out your salvation with fear and*** *trembling."* In the old days, a doctor's word was the final word. In modern days patients are armed with knowledge and can get a second opinion while leaving the parking lot. In the same way, Jesus died so that you do not need a priest to come to God. An intimate relationship with God must become a daily priority in your life. Likewise take responsibility for your deliverance. It's your life. You know what you have suffered in the hands of familiar spirits. A familiar spirit fears an informed believer, with prayer power to keep them at bay.

Determine to connect with God today. So what about church? The answer is easier answered now than ever before. There are many ways to attend services. I suggest finding a ministry you enjoy and attending live services online for now. Seek God during this time for the right church that will nurture your growth in the Lord. Reach out to the ministry team of that church for a consultation or counseling.

If you fall into the category of those who have been broken in churches due to the antics of familiar spirits, or you have major trust issues because of satanic ritual abuse or some of the other atrocities that these spirits have sponsored. I suggest you develop a deliverance by-all-means mentality. If you feel entirely too traumatized to meet with a minister, then you must consider self-deliverance and strong prayer ministry. I will list what I consider to be very helpful reading in the addendum. I believe that you will reclaim your life in the name of Jesus Christ.

So what is the big deal about deliverance? Deliverance is crucial because familiar spirits, especially in witchcraft, specialize in isolating and separating people. The English Standard Version of Proverbs 16:28 states "A dishonest man spreads strife, and a whisperer separates close friends." Who else whispers and mutters? You got it, familiar spirits. If you can find one Christian believer you trust to join faith with you, then you can be free. If the witchcraft of familiar spirits has driven everyone away, you are not without hope. Exercise the spiritual law of legal rights and agree with the Word of God. I will list an entire section of scriptures designed for deliverance. Read at least one each day and completely agree with everything you read. Satan and his angels have employed various technologies and legal grounds to bring you into bondage, therefore you have legal grounds to apply the same to be free. The Word of God will give you those legal grounds. Your first agreement partner is always our father God, who agreed to your freedom. So let's do an exercise. If possible get on your knees. Feel the presence of the Lord and simply say, "Sister Zion wrote in her book that you are ready and waiting to agree with me to be set free. I have made some mistakes, will you agree with me for my freedom? Now feel the answer.

<u>Yahweh's Answer To You</u>

American King James Version

"For thus said the LORD, You have sold yourselves for nothing; and you shall be redeemed without money." Isn't that great news. You may have unknowingly sold your joy and peace to familiar spirits but the most high God will restore you. He agrees with your deliverance. Hallelujah.

Isaiah 49:8-9

This is what the LORD says:

"In the time of favor I will answer You, and in the day of salvation I will help You; I will keep You and appoint You to be a covenant for the people, to restore the land, to apportion its desolate inheritances, 9. To say to the prisoners, 'Come out,' and to those in darkness, 'Show yourselves.'

Isaiah 49: 23-25

"Then you will know that I am the LORD;t those who hope in Me will never be put to shame."

Can the plunder be snatched from the mighty, or the captives of a tyrant be delivered?

Indeed, this is what the LORD says: "Even the captives of the mighty will be taken away, and the plunder of the tyrant will be retrieved;

I will contend with those who contend with you, and I will save your children.

I will make your oppressors eat their flesh; they will be drunk on their own blood, as with wine.

Then all mankind will know that I, the LORD, am your Savior and your Redeemer, the Mighty One of Jacob."

Who are the mighty? The evil familiar spirits and their cohorts! You are already ahead of many people who pray amiss and the Lord ignores their prayers. Now you have established the most powerful prayer partner that anyone could ever dream of having. There are some other people want who want to join your team.

Your Next Team Member

Jesus, who, according to Colossians 2:9 said, "For in Christ lives all the fullness of God in a human body." What a resume!

He says

Luke 4:18

"The Spirit of the Lord is upon me, because he has anointed me to proclaim good news to the poor has sent me to proclaim liberty to the captives and recovering of sight to the blind, to set at liberty those who are oppressed, to proclaim the year of the Lord's favor."

Jesus not only wants to agree with you but he wants to take that agreement and deliver you from the familiar spirit tormenting your life.

Your Third Team Member

The Holy Ghost is also interested in teaming with you for deliverance.

2 Corinthians 3

"Now the **Lord** is the **Spirit**, and where the **Spirit of the Lord is, there** is freedom. And we, who with unveiled faces all reflect the **Lord's** glory, are being transformed into his likeness with ever–increasing glory, which comes from the **Lord**, who is the **Spirit**."

<u>Additional Team Members</u>

The Holy Angels also agree with your deliverance

Luke 15:10

"Likewise, I say unto you, there is joy in the presence of the angels of God over one sinner that repenteth."

Psalm 91:10-12

There shall no evil befall thee, neither shall any plague come nigh thy dwelling.

11 For he shall give his angels charge over thee, to keep thee in all thy ways.

12 They shall bear thee up in their hands, lest thou dash thy foot against a stone.

Intercessors all over the world are agreeing with your deliverance. I agree with your deliverance. You have a powerful team that wants you to survive and overcome the onslaught of familiar spirits. You are not alone. I suggest you complete the worksheets at the end of this book and pray diligently. I also suggest that you visit the websites, and purchase the books suggested in the appendix. Every time you purchase a book or spend time working on self-deliverance you are investing in your freedom. How many things have you purchased to cope with the pain these evil spirits have caused your life?

Familiar Spirits can be stubborn. They will certainly try to return when cast out. You must maintain your deliverance. Maintaining your deliverance is requires a commitment to your salvation.

1. Read your Bible and learn what God says about your freedom.

2. Participate in aggressive praise and worship sessions.

3. Pray like your life depends on it. It does.

4. Fasting is feasting with God. Some spirits will turn a deaf ear to anyone who has not fasted.

5. Evaluate your relationships. If you discern a spiritually or physically harmful person, seek the Lord for the best way to address that relationship. This is especially true when witchcraft is present.

6. Remember the veil was torn. Trust God to heal you and show you the right church to join. Do not wait for the pastor to discern your needs. If you are led to a church during the deliverance process, meet with your pastor so they

can help in your deliverance by laying hands and combining faith. They may also have special insights or receive words of wisdom or words of knowledge concerning your specific circumstances

7. Deliverance is an ongoing process. Be willing to revisit deliverance whenever you feel it is necessary.

When you have developed a lifestyle of hearing God, ask him to show you the right church. Enter your church an informed and vibrant saint and work diligently to win souls and grow in the Lord.

Do not wait to be perfect to go to church. The point is not to expose yourself to unnecessary spiritual harm. not to stay out of church waiting to be perfectly demon-free.

9

The Word of God on Deliverance

Deliverance is possible with the Word of God. Jesus said, "Heal the sick, cleanse the lepers, raise the dead, cast out devils: freely ye have received, freely give." You can be free. Receive deliverance by the Word of God.

2 Kings 17:39
   But the Lord your God ye shall fear, and he shall deliver you out of the hand of all your enemies

Exodus 3:8
   And I am come down to deliver them out of the hand of the Egyptians, and to bring them up out of that land unto a good land and a large, unto a land flowing with milk and honey; unto the place of the Canaanites, and the Hittites, and the Amorites, and the Perizzites, and the Hivites, and the Jebusites

Deuteronomy 32:39
   See now that I, even I, am he, and there is no god with me: I kill, and I make alive; I wound, and I heal: neither is there any that can deliver out of my hand

Judges 8:34
   And the children of Israel remembered not the Lord their God, who had delivered them out of the hands of all their enemies on every

1 Samuel 17:46

This day will the Lord deliver thee into mine hand; and I will smite thee, and take thine head from thee; and I will give the carcases of the host of the Philistines this day unto the fowls of the air, and to the wild beasts of the earth; that all the earth may know that there is a God in Israel

2 Samuel 22:2

And he said, The Lord is my rock, and my fortress, and my deliverer;

2 Samuel 22:18

He delivered me from my strong enemy, and from them that hated me: for they were too strong for me.

2 Samuel 22:20

He brought me forth also into a large place: he delivered me, because he delighted in me.

2 Samuel 22:44

Thou also hast delivered me from the strivings of my people, thou hast kept me to be head of the heathen: a people which I knew not shall serve me.

2 Samuel 22:49

And that bringeth me forth from mine enemies: thou also hast lifted me up on high above them that rose up against me: thou hast delivered me from the violent man.

1 Kings 20:28

And there came a man of God, and spake unto the king of Israel, and said, Thus saith the Lord, Because the Syrians have said, The Lord is God of the hills, but he is not God of the valleys, therefore will I deliver all this great multitude into thine hand, and ye shall know that I am the Lord

2 Kings 17:39

But the Lord your God ye shall fear; and he shall deliver you out of the hand of all your enemies

Job 5:19

He shall deliver thee in six troubles: yea, in seven there shall no evil touch thee

Job 36:15

He delivereth the poor in his affliction, and openeth their ears in oppression

Psalm 17:13

Arise, O Lord, disappoint him, cast him down: deliver my soul from the wicked, which is thy sword:

Psalm 18:2

The Lord is my rock, and my fortress, and my deliverer; my God, my strength, in whom I will trust; my buckler, and the horn of my salvation, and my high tower.

Psalm 18:17

He delivered me from my strong enemy, and from them which hated me: for they were too strong for me.

Psalm 18:19

He brought me forth also into a large place; he delivered me, because he delighted in me.

Psalm 18:43

Thou hast delivered me from the strivings of the people; and thou hast made me the head of the heathen: a people whom I have not known shall serve me.

Psalm 18:48

He delivereth me from mine enemies: yea, thou liftest me up above those that rise up against me: thou hast delivered me from the violent man.

Psalm 18:50

Great deliverance giveth he to his king; and sheweth mercy to his anointed, to David, and to his seed for evermore.

Psalm 22:4

Our fathers trusted in thee: they trusted, and thou didst deliver them.

Psalm 22:5

They cried unto thee, and were delivered: they trusted in thee, and were not confounded.

Psalm 22:8

He trusted on the Lord that he would deliver him: let him deliver him, seeing he delighted in him.

Psalm 22:20

Deliver my soul from the sword; my darling from the power of the dog.

Psalm 25:20

O keep my soul, and deliver me: let me not be ashamed; for I put my trust in thee.

Psalm 27:12

Deliver me not over unto the will of mine enemies: for false witnesses are risen up against me, and such as breathe out cruelty.

Psalm 31:1

In thee, O Lord, do I put my trust; let me never be ashamed: deliver me in thy righteousness.

Psalm 31:2
Bow down thine ear to me; deliver me speedily: be thou my strong rock, for an house of defence to save me.

Psalm 31:15
My times are in thy hand: deliver me from the hand of mine enemies, and from them that persecute me.

Psalm 32:7
Thou art my hiding place; thou shalt preserve me from trouble; thou shalt compass me about with songs of deliverance. Selah.

Psalm 33:16
There is no king saved by the multitude of an host: a mighty man is not delivered by much strength.

Psalm 33:17
An horse is a vain thing for safety: neither shall he deliver any by his great strength.

Psalm 33:19
To deliver their soul from death, and to keep them alive in famine.

Psalm 34:4
I sought the Lord, and he heard me, and delivered me from all my fears.

Psalm 34:7
The angel of the Lord encampeth round about them that fear him, and delivereth them.

Psalm 34:17

The righteous cry, and the Lord heareth, and delivereth them out of all their troubles.

Psalm 34:19

Many are the afflictions of the righteous: but the Lord delivereth him out of them all.

Psalm 35:10

All my bones shall say, Lord, who is like unto thee, which deliverest the poor from him that is too strong for him, yea, the poor and the needy from him that spoileth him?

Psalm 37:40

And the Lord shall help them, and deliver them: he shall deliver them from the wicked, and save them, because they trust in him.

Psalm 39:8

Deliver me from all my transgressions: make me not the reproach of the foolish.

Psalm 40:13

Be pleased, O Lord, to deliver me: O Lord, make haste to help me.

Psalm 40:17

But I am poor and needy; yet the Lord thinketh upon me: thou art my help and my deliverer; make no tarrying, O my God.

Psalm 41:1

Blessed is he that considereth the poor: the Lord will deliver him in time of trouble.

Psalm 41:2

The Lord will preserve him, and keep him alive; and he shall be blessed upon the earth: and thou wilt not deliver him unto the will of his enemies.

Psalm 43:1

Judge me, O God, and plead my cause against an ungodly nation: O deliver me from the deceitful and unjust man.

Psalm 44:4

Thou art my King, O God: command deliverances for Jacob.

Psalm 50:15

And call upon me in the day of trouble: I will deliver thee, and thou shalt glorify me.

Psalm 50:22

Now consider this, ye that forget God, lest I tear you in pieces, and there be none to deliver.

Psalm 51:14

Deliver me from bloodguiltiness, O God, thou God of my salvation: and my tongue shall sing aloud of thy righteousness.

Psalm 54:7

For he hath delivered me out of all trouble: and mine eye hath seen his desire upon mine enemies.

Psalm 55:18

He hath delivered my soul in peace from the battle that was against me: for there were many with me.

Psalm 56:13

For thou hast delivered my soul from death: wilt not thou deliver my feet from falling, that I may walk before God in the light of the living?

Psalm 59:1

Deliver me from mine enemies, O my God: defend me from them that rise up against me.

Psalm 59:2

Deliver me from the workers of iniquity, and save me from bloody men.

Psalm 60:5

That thy beloved may be delivered; save with thy right hand, and hear me.

Psalm 69:14

Deliver me out of the mire, and let me not sink: let me be delivered from them that hate me, and out of the deep waters.

Psalm 69:18

Draw nigh unto my soul, and redeem it: deliver me because of mine enemies.

Psalm 70:1

Make haste, o God, to deliver me; make haste to help me, O Lord.

Psalm 70:5

But I am poor and needy: make haste unto me, O God: thou art my help and my deliverer; O Lord, make no tarrying.

Psalm 71:2

Deliver me in thy righteousness, and cause me to escape: incline thine ear unto me, and save me.

Psalm 71:4

Deliver me, O my God, out of the hand of the wicked, out of the hand of the unrighteous and cruel man.

Psalm 71:11

Saying, God hath forsaken him: persecute and take him; for there is none to deliver him.

Psalm 72:12

For he shall deliver the needy when he crieth; the poor also, and him that hath no helper.

Psalm 74:19

O deliver not the soul of thy turtledove unto the multitude of the wicked: forget not the congregation of thy poor for ever.

Psalm 78:42

They remembered not his hand, nor the day when he delivered them from the enemy.

Psalm 78:61

And delivered his strength into captivity, and his glory into the enemy's hand.

Psalm 79:9

Help us, O God of our salvation, for the glory of thy name: and deliver us, and purge away our sins, for thy name's sake.

Psalm 81:6

I removed his shoulder from the burden: his hands were delivered from the pots.

Psalm 81:7

Thou calledst in trouble, and I delivered thee; I answered thee in the secret place of thunder: I proved thee at the waters of Meribah. Selah.

Psalm 82:4

Deliver the poor and needy: rid them out of the hand of the wicked.

Psalm 86:13

For great is thy mercy toward me: and thou hast delivered my soul from the lowest hell.

Psalm 89:48

What man is he that liveth, and shall not see death? shall he deliver his soul from the hand of the grave? Selah.

Psalm 91:3

Surely he shall deliver thee from the snare of the fowler, and from the noisome pestilence.

Psalm 91:14

Because he hath set his love upon me, therefore will I deliver him: I will set him on high, because he hath known my name

Psalm 91:15

He shall call upon me, and I will answer him: I will be with him in trouble; I will deliver him, and honour him.

Psalm 97:10

Ye that love the Lord, hate evil: he preserveth the souls of his saints; he delivereth them out of the hand of the wicked.

Psalm 106:43

Many times did he deliver them; but they provoked him with their counsel, and were brought low for their iniquity.

Psalm 107:6

Then they cried unto the Lord in their trouble, and he delivered them out of their distresses.

Psalm 107:20

He sent his word, and healed them, and delivered them from their destructions.

Psalm 108:6

That thy beloved may be delivered: save with thy right hand, and answer me.

Psalm 109:21

But do thou for me, O God the Lord, for thy name's sake: because thy mercy is good, deliver thou me.

Psalm 116:4

Then called I upon the name of the Lord; O Lord, I beseech thee, deliver my soul.

Psalm 116:8

For thou hast delivered my soul from death, mine eyes from tears, and my feet from falling.

Psalm 119:134

Deliver me from the oppression of man: so will I keep thy precepts.

Psalm 119:153

Consider mine affliction, and deliver me: for I do not forget thy law.

Psalm 119:154

Plead my cause, and deliver me: quicken me according to thy word.

Psalm 119:170

Let my supplication come before thee: deliver me according to thy word.

Psalm 120:2

Deliver my soul, O Lord, from lying lips, and from a deceitful tongue.

Psalm 140:1

Deliver me, O Lord, from the evil man: preserve me from the violent man;

Psalm 142:6

Attend unto my cry; for I am brought very low: deliver me from my persecutors; for they are stronger than I.

Psalm 143:9

Deliver me, O Lord, from mine enemies: I flee unto thee to hide me.

Psalm 144:2

My goodness, and my fortress; my high tower, and my deliverer; my shield, and he in whom I trust; who subdueth my people under me.

Psalm 144:7

Send thine hand from above; rid me, and deliver me out of great waters, from the hand of strange children;

Psalm 144:10

It is he that giveth salvation unto kings: who delivereth David his servant from the hurtful sword.

Psalm 144:11

Rid me, and deliver me from the hand of strange children, whose mouth speaketh vanity, and their right hand is a right hand of falsehood:

Proverbs 2:12

To deliver thee from the way of the evil man, from the man that speaketh froward things;

Proverbs 2:16

To deliver thee from the strange woman, even from the stranger which flattereth with her words;

Proverbs 10:2
Treasures of wickedness profit nothing: but righteousness delivereth from death.

Proverbs 11:4
Riches profit not in the day of wrath: but righteousness delivereth from death.

Proverbs 11:6
The righteousness of the upright shall deliver them: but transgressors shall be taken in their own naughtiness.

Proverbs 11:8
The righteous is delivered out of trouble, and the wicked cometh in his stead.

Proverbs 11:9
An hypocrite with his mouth destroyeth his neighbour: but through knowledge shall the just be delivered.

Proverbs 11:21
Though hand join in hand, the wicked shall not be unpunished: but the seed of the righteous shall be delivered.

Proverbs 12:6
The words of the wicked are to lie in wait for blood: but the mouth of the upright shall deliver them.

Isaiah 19:20
And it shall be for a sign and for a witness unto the Lord of hosts in the land of Egypt: for they shall cry unto the Lord because of the oppressors, and he

shall send them a saviour, and a great one, and he shall deliver them

Isaiah 38:17

Behold, for peace I had great bitterness: but thou hast in love to my soul delivered it from the pit of corruption: for thou hast cast all my sins behind thy back

Isaiah 46:4

And even to your old age I am he; and even to hoar hairs will I carry you: I have made, and I will bear; even I will carry, and will deliver you.

Isaiah 49:24

Shall the prey be taken from the mighty, or the lawful captive delivered?

Isaiah 49:25

But thus saith the Lord, Even the captives of the mighty shall be taken away, and the prey of the terrible shall be delivered: for I will contend with him that contendeth with thee, and I will save thy children.

Isaiah 50:2

Wherefore, when I came, was there no man? when I called, was there none to answer? Is my hand shortened at all, that it cannot redeem? or have I no power to deliver? behold, at my rebuke I dry up the sea, I make the rivers a wilderness: their fish stinketh, because there is no water, and dieth for thirst.

Jeremiah 1:8

Be not afraid of their faces: for I am with thee to deliver thee, saith the Lord.

Jeremiah 1:19

And they shall fight against thee; but they shall not prevail against thee; for I am with thee, saith the Lord, to deliver thee.

Jeremiah 15:20

And I will make thee unto this people a fenced brasen wall: and they shall fight against thee, but they shall not prevail against thee: for I am with thee to save thee and to deliver thee, saith the Lord

Jeremiah 15:21

And I will deliver thee out of the hand of the wicked, and I will redeem thee out of the hand of the terrible.

Jeremiah 20:13

Sing unto the Lord, praise ye the Lord: for he hath delivered the soul of the poor from the hand of evildoers.

Jeremiah 21:12

O house of David, thus saith the Lord; Execute judgment in the morning, and deliver him that is spoiled out of the hand of the oppressor, lest my fury go out like fire, and burn that none can quench it, because of the evil of your doings.

Jeremiah 22:3

Thus saith the Lord; Execute ye judgment and righteousness, and deliver the spoiled out of the hand of the oppressor: and do no wrong, do no violence to the stranger, the fatherless, nor the widow, neither shed innocent blood in this place.

Ezekiel 13:21

Your kerchiefs also will I tear, and deliver my people out of your hand, and they shall be no more in your hand to be hunted; and ye shall know that I am the Lord.

Ezekiel 13:23

Therefore ye shall see no more vanity, nor divine divinations: for I will deliver my people out of your hand: and ye shall know that I am the LordEzekiel

34:10

Thus saith the Lord God; Behold, I am against the shepherds; and I will require my flock at their hand, and cause them to cease from feeding the flock; neither shall the shepherds feed themselves any more; for I will deliver my flock from their mouth, that they may not be meat for them

Ezekiel 34:1

As a shepherd seeketh out his flock in the day that he is among his sheep that are scattered; so will I seek out my sheep, and will deliver them out of all places where they have been scattered in the cloudy and dark day

Ezekiel 34:2

And the tree of the field shall yield her fruit, and the earth shall yield her increase, and they shall be safe in their land, and shall know that I am the Lord, when I have broken the bands of their yoke, and delivered them out of the hand of those that served themselves of them7s.2s.

Daniel 6:27

He delivereth and rescueth, and he worketh signs and wonders in heaven and in earth, who hath delivered Daniel from the power of the lions.

Daniel 12:1

And at that time shall Michael stand up, the great prince which standeth for the children of thy people: and there shall be a time of trouble, such as never was since there was a nation even to that same time: and at that time thy people shall be delivered, every one that shall be found written in the book

Joel 2:32

And it shall come to pass, that whosoever shall call on the name of the Lord shall be delivered: for in mount Zion and in Jerusalem shall be deliverance, as the Lord hath said, and in the remnant whom the Lord shall call.

Obadiah 1:17

But upon mount Zion shall be deliverance, and there shall be holiness; and the house of Jacob shall possess their possessions

Matthew 6:13

And lead us not into temptation, but deliver us from evil: For thine is the kingdom, and the power, and the glory, for ever. Amen

Luke 1:74

That he would grant unto us, that we being delivered out of the hand of our enemies might serve him without fear

Luke 4:18

The Spirit of the Lord is upon me, because he hath anointed me to preach the gospel to the poor; he hath sent me to heal the brokenhearted, to preach deliverance to the captives, and recovering of sight to the blind, to set at liberty them that are bruised

Luke 7:15

And he that was dead sat up, and began to speak. And he delivered him to his mother.

Luke 9:42

And as he was yet a coming, the devil threw him down, and tare him. And Jesus rebuked the unclean spirit, and healed the child, and delivered him again to his father

Romans 7:24

O wretched man that I am! who shall deliver me from the body of this death?

Romans 8:21

Because the creature itself also shall be delivered from the bondage of corruption into the glorious liberty of the children of God.

Romans 8:32

He that spared not his own Son, but delivered him up for us all, how shall he not with him also freely give us all things?

Romans 11:26

And so all Israel shall be saved: as it is written, There shall come out of Sion the Deliverer, and shall turn away ungodliness from Jacob

Galatians 1:4

Who gave himself for our sins, that he might deliver us from this present evil world, according to the will of God and our Father

Colossians 1:13

Who hath delivered us from the power of darkness, and hath translated us into the kingdom of his dear Son:

1 Thessalonians 1:10

And to wait for his Son from heaven, whom he raised from the dead, even Jesus, which delivered us from the wrath to come.

2 Thessalonians 3:2

And that we may be delivered from unreasonable and wicked men: for all men have not faith.

2 Timothy 4:18

And the Lord shall deliver me from every evil work, and will preserve me unto his heavenly kingdom: to whom be glory for ever and ever. Amen.

Hebrews 2:15

And deliver them who through fear of death were all their lifetime subject to bondage.

2 Peter 2:9

The Lord knoweth how to deliver the godly out of temptations, and to reserve the unjust unto the day of judgment to be punished:

2 Peter 2:21

For it had been better for them not to have known the way of righteousness, than, after they have known it, to turn from the holy commandment delivered unto them.

<u>Cast out</u>

Matthew 10:8

Heal the sick, cleanse the lepers, raise the dead, cast out devils: freely ye have received, freely give.

Deuteronomy 6:19

To cast out all thine enemies from before thee, as the Lord hath spoken

Zephaniah 3:15

The Lord hath taken away thy judgments, he hath cast out thine enemy: the king of Israel, even the Lord, is in the midst of thee: thou shalt not see evil any more.

Matthew 7:22

Many will say to me in that day, Lord, Lord, have we not prophesied in thy name? and in thy name have cast out devils? and in thy name done many wonderful works?

Matthew 8:16

When the even was come, they brought unto him many that were possessed with devils: and he cast out the spirits with his word, and healed all that were sick:

In Context | Full Chapter | Other Translations

Matthew 8:31

So the devils besought him, saying, If thou cast us out, suffer us to go away into the herd of swine.

In Context | Full Chapter | Other Translations

Matthew 9:33

And when the devil was cast out, the dumb spake: and the multitudes marvelled, saying, It was never so seen in Israel.

In Context | Full Chapter | Other Translations

Matthew 9:34

But the Pharisees said, He casteth out devils through the prince of the devils.

In Context | Full Chapter | Other Translations

Matthew 10:1

And when he had called unto him his twelve disciples, he gave them power against unclean spirits, to cast them out, and to heal all manner of sickness and all manner of disease.

In Context | Full Chapter | Other Translations

Matthew 10:8

Heal the sick, cleanse the lepers, raise the dead, cast out devils: freely ye have received, freely give.

In Context | Full Chapter | Other Translations

Matthew 12:24

But when the Pharisees heard it, they said, This fellow doth not cast out devils, but by Beelzebub the prince of the devils.

In Context | Full Chapter | Other Translations

Matthew 12:26

And if Satan cast out Satan, he is divided against himself; how shall then his kingdom stand?

In Context | Full Chapter | Other Translations

Matthew 12:27

And if I by Beelzebub cast out devils, by whom do your children cast them out? therefore they shall be your judges.

In Context | Full Chapter | Other Translations

Matthew 12:28

But if I cast out devils by the Spirit of God, then the kingdom of God is come unto you.

In Context | Full Chapter | Other Translations

Matthew 15:17

Do not ye yet understand, that whatsoever entereth in at the mouth goeth into the belly, and is cast out into the draught?

In Context | Full Chapter | Other Translations

Matthew 17:19

Then came the disciples to Jesus apart, and said, Why could not we cast him out?

In Context | Full Chapter | Other

Mark 1:34

And he healed many that were sick of divers diseases, and cast out many devils; and suffered not the devils to speak, because they knew him.

In Context | Full Chapter | Other Translations

Mark 1:39

And he preached in their synagogues throughout all Galilee, and cast out devils.

In Context | Full Chapter | Other Translations

Mark 3:15

And to have power to heal sicknesses, and to cast out devils:

In Context | Full Chapter | Other Translations

Mark 3:22

And the scribes which came down from Jerusalem said, He hath Beelzebub, and by the prince of the devils casteth he out devils.

In Context | Full Chapter | Other Translations

Mark 3:23

And he called them unto him, and said unto them in parables, How can Satan cast out Satan?

In Context | Full Chapter | Other Translations

Mark 6:13

And they cast out many devils, and anointed with oil many that were sick, and healed them.

In Context | Full Chapter | Other Translations

Mark 7:26

The woman was a Greek, a Syrophenician by nation; and she besought him that he would cast forth the devil out of her daughter.

In Context | Full Chapter | Other Translations

Mark 9:18

And wheresoever he taketh him, he teareth him: and he foameth, and gnasheth with his teeth, and pineth away: and I spake to thy disciples that they should cast him out; and they could not.

Mark 9:28

And when he was come into the house, his disciples asked him privately, Why could not we cast him out?

In Context | Full Chapter | Other Translations

Mark 9:38

And John answered him, saying, Master, we saw one casting out devils in thy name, and he followeth not us: and we forbad him, because he followeth not us.

Mark 16:17

And these signs shall follow them that believe; In my name shall they cast out devils; they shall speak with new tongues.

Luke 11:14

And he was casting out a devil, and it was dumb. And it came to pass, when the devil was gone out, the dumb spake; and the people wondered.

In Context | Full Chapter | Other Translations

Luke 11:15

But some of them said, He casteth out devils through Beelzebub the chief of the devils.

In Context | Full Chapter | Other Translations

Luke 11:18

If Satan also be divided against himself, how shall his kingdom stand? because ye say that I cast out devils through Beelzebub.

In Context | Full Chapter | Other Translations

Luke 11:19

And if I by Beelzebub cast out devils, by whom do your sons cast them out? therefore shall they be your judges.

In Context | Full Chapter | Other Translations

Luke 11:20

But if I with the finger of God cast out devils, no doubt the kingdom of God is come upon you.

In Context | Full Chapter | Other Translations

Luke 13:32

And he said unto them, Go ye, and tell that fox, Behold, I cast out devils, and I do cures to day and to morrow, and the third day I shall be perfected.

Revelation 12:9

And the great dragon was cast out, that old serpent, called the Devil, and Satan, which deceiveth the whole world: he was cast out into the earth, and his angels were cast out with him.

10

Addendum

Symptoms of Familiar Spirits Manipulation

- -Are you constantly harassed in your dreams?
- -Have you noticed a persistent problem that affects all members, of a certain sex in your family?
- -Have you had dreams or heard voices stating that they are your spouse?
- -Do you have a family history of witchcraft, secret societies such as Freemason, Eastern Star, or Shriners?
- - Have you or your family members been involved with Mormons, Scientology, Islam, or Buddhism?
- - Have you ever taken a blood oath?
- -Have you ever had an association or committed any act of fornication or lust with anyone who could be involved in witchcraft, the occult, or secret societies?
- -Is your life repeating the same cycle?
- -Did your ancestors commit atrocities against anyone?
- - Do you have regular cycles of financial troubles, sickness, or repeated issues?

Each item indicates the presence of a familiar spirit. It is not unusual to have several of these situations at work. Spirits work to create as many legal rights as possible.

List of battle scriptures

Genesis 1:3-4
   Isaiah 54:17
   James 4:7
   Psalm 109
   2 Corinthians 10:3-5
   Nahum 1:1-11
   Obadiah 1:15-17

Reading List
   *Please note. I am not affiliated in any way with the authors of the books or creator of the website. These are tools that I suggest to perfect your freedom.

Win Worley- Battling the hosts of hell

DK Olukoya- Prayer Rain

Win Worley- How Demons Operate

He Came To Set The Captives Free- Dr. Rebecca Brown Yoder

Destroying The Works of Witchcraft Through Fasting and Prayer- Ruth Brown

Demonbuster
   www.demonbuster.com

How to Obtain Personal Deliverance- Dr. DK Olukoya

They Shall Expel Demons- Derek Prince

11

Blessed Assurance

Blessed assurance, Jesus is mine;
  Oh, what a foretaste of glory divine!
  Heir of salvation, purchase of God,
  Born of His Spirit, washed in His blood.

This is my story, this is my song,
  Praising my Savior all the day long.
  This is my story, this is my song,
  Praising my Savior all the day long.

Perfect submission, perfect delight,
  Visions of rapture now burst on my sight;
  Angels descending, bring from above
  Echoes of mercy, whispers of love.

Perfect submission, all is at rest,
  I in my Savior am happy and blest;
  Watching and waiting, looking above,
  Filled with His goodness, lost in His love

You have a blessed assurance of Jesus today. He wants you to walk in freedom. Praise God that you can, and you will be filled with his goodness and list in his love.

About the Author

Zion Willingham is the author of Trigger Warning, Natural Health and Divine Healing, Take Your Life Back from Familiar Spirits, and the Battle Plan series. She has a unique focus on prayer with special attention to individuals with deep soul wounds and abuse.

Zion Willingham is the prophetic voice behind Sanctuary Prayer Ministries.

Sanctuary Prayer Ministries is a ministry that exists with the sole purpose of seeking God in prayer and fulfilling the great mandate. We only have one agenda, and that is to pray and study the Word of God. Catch our podcast on Monday, Wednesday, and Saturday. You can also hear a Word from God Sundays at 7 pm. Visit our websites for more information.

You can connect with me on:

🌐 https://sanctuaryprayerministries.wordpress.com

🔗 https://parentsarms.com

Also by Zion Willingham

Check out our other spirit-filled books.

Self-Deliverance Manual

What do you do when you need freedom and there is no one available to help? What do you do when the amount of satanic concentration against your life is so thick that Pastors dare not help, for fear of the backlash? What do you do when the enemy has separated you from friends and family, and you can't find one person to agree with you? What do you do when your presence brings irritation and attacks to anyone you come into contact with? What do you do when unexplained demonic activities invade your home? The answer is simple, the method may not be. Deliverance is the answer. So what do you do when there is none to deliver? The good news is that Jesus Christ will deliver you.

The Holy Spirit brings about deliverance through yielded human beings. Therefore it stands to reason that if the extension cord is missing, you will need to plug yourself directly into the outlet of power. Will it be easy? It may or may not be easy. Deliverance can be compared to delivering a baby. It may be hard, long, and involve a lot of effort and pain, or it can be quick and easy. Either way, the results are worth the effort.

In his song, Hear the footsteps of Jesus, William J Kirkpatrick asked, Wilt thou be made whole" The question still lingers today. Do you hear Jesus calling you to be made whole?

Faith Is...

Do you know faith? This is not a typo. Do you know faith? Is faith a spirit, or a state of mind. Is faith an emotion or a feeling. Can faith be touched, felt, experienced by the average person. How about the unsaved? Can an unbeliever have faith? How about an agent of darkness? What can faith do for your life? In this book Zion Willingham takes a holistic approach to the subject of faith.

Finding The Missing Coin

Where is your missing coin? Do you feel like you have lost things that should make you great? Are you clueless to where to find them, or how to get them back. We will discuss the way coins are lost and the methods the enemy employs to steal our coins

Your Life TRANSFORMED

God wants to talk to you. God wants to talk through you. He wants a deeper walk with you. He wants to grow your faith. He wants to increase your annointing and break the yokes in your life. He wants to save your marriage, guide you in your career, perform miraculous feats of healing and miracles, or simply guide you in your day to day life. You need to interact with the Holy Spirit! This could be the most pivotal thirty days of your life. He is standing at the door and knocking. Will you answer?

Arise to Manifest

We review the five-fold ministry in this series of five booklets

For The Love of God

Do you remember the old-time hymns? Sings that take you to a deep place. Songs you sing for the Love of God.

This is a thirty-day devotional with hymns, scriptures, and a statement for each day. Join Zion Willingham as she explores living for the Love of God.

Natural Health and Divine Healing Three Book Series

Battle Plan Series

Four Book Battle Prayer Series